Woman:
Splendor and Sorrow

Love Poems and Poetic Prose

Gabriela Marie Milton

ISBN: 978-1-7372965-0-8

Image used in the cover: Odalisque in a modern style - original acrylic painting by arteliia (Shutterstock)

Dedication

My Dear Readers,

This book is dedicated to my family, whom I love deeply, and to you.

My favorite novelist, Lawrence Durrell, once asked:

"Who invented the human heart, I wonder? Tell me, and then show me the place where he was hanged."

If you read this book, you will find that place. Yet make no mistake. That is not a sad place. In the pages you are about to read, I resurrect the one who invented the human heart. The splendors of candlelight and roses and the taste of gingerbread dwell in this book. Partake in them.

The core of this book is love. Yet you will also find in it philosophical thoughts on literature, on winning and losing, on hate, on feminism, and on life in general.

My dear reader, from wherever you are in this world, walk with me on the beautiful path of the human heart. I promise you will not regret doing so. On this road you will find love and the symbols that define us as humans.

Sincerely,

Gabriela Marie Milton
2019 Author of the Year at Spillwords Press, NYC
Author of *Passions: Love Poems and Other Writings* (*Vita Brevis Press*, 2020)

Table of Contents

"It is this admirable, this immortal, instinctive sense of beauty that leads us to look upon the spectacle of this world as a glimpse, a correspondence with heaven. Our unquenchable thirst for all that lies beyond, and that life reveals, is the liveliest proof of our immortality. It is both by poetry and through poetry…that the soul dimly descries the splendours beyond the tomb; and when an exquisite poem brings tears to our eyes, those tears are not a proof of overabundant joy: they bear witness rather to an impatient melancholy, a clamant demand by our nerves, our nature, exiled in imperfection, which would fain enter into immediate possession, while still on this earth, of a revealed paradise."

— Charles Baudelaire, Selected Writings on Art and Literature

Foreword

A poem in itself is a marvelous thing, but a collection of poetry is something else entirely — like the broader beauty of an arabesque, it's felt more than seen. Perhaps this is what T.S. Elliot meant when he said genuine poetry communicates before it's understood. The nebulous beauty of art, the feelings it stirs before we parse it for meaning, sometimes finds the world with more precision than instruments of any other sort.

This is what you'll find in Gabriela Marie Milton's poetry collection, *Woman: Splendor and Sorrow*. It's an arabesque of womanhood, depicting the broad strokes and finer details of love, identity, and femininity. With vibrant imagery and fresh ideas, Milton's poetry and prose explore these topics with passion and sincerity. There's something here for all readers.

Brian Geiger
editor of Vita Brevis Press

Love Poems

The Easter of Roses

my love
you know that spring will come
peaches will grow on one side of the moon
injured lambs will scream on the other
taste of strawberries
my hair freshly cut
possessed by new ghosts will look for each other
steps on the asphalt heard from cafes
the baptism of rain and thin yellow candles
a verse from Seferis hangs on your lips
the Easter of Roses with its cold morning showers
never to sin your hands nailed in white marble
the rode of your anchor
my love
it's spring
it's me
free your hands from the marble

Daughter of this Earth

inside the altars of the churches with blue cupolas
he recounts the spring cuckoo's notes
his cries strip him of himself
modify his flesh until the days are born from the wounds of his feet
daughter of this earth
I can hear his bones cracking with love for you
his voice made from curses and myrrh
his body stretched between heaven and the bloom of the olive trees
his retina caught inside the limonite of the yellow marble
everything speaks of the impossibility of tomorrow
daughter of this earth
you
who travel in the lands of the snakes with no name
and shed your skin and your beauty in every sunset
you are the virginal sin in the nights of the hyacinths
show mercy
go back to him
the resurrection is near

Professions

Motto: I get drunk on love, charity, and passion.
These are my professions.

I walk into the three days we spent together.

On the first day, a nude silence wraps around my lips. Shortly after
I can hear the noise of wine poured into glasses.
The hour to get drunk on love has come.
I touch your skin and another you is born.
Birds invade the sky.
A banquet of candles floods the streets.
A white thread ties my blood vessels at the exact moment when a
religious procession walks by.

On the second day, drunk on charity, my sights descend upon the
earth.
The dirty hands of the woman who owns wells touch my skin.
I hear your voice.
I will not counsel her or belittle her desires.
All she will do is sell her fake dreams in the corner of an empty
street for her entire life.
I forbid you.
By punishing her, you would have ruined the very thing you set
out to safeguard: our love.

On the third day, stars melt in our palms like soft grapes in
winepresses.
The intimations of you and I, with their smell and softness of grass
and late autumn roses, invade the room.
A convulsive joy impregnates your eyes.

Words have no pigments and no form.

Their register sinks in gravity, shiny coil by shiny coil, musical key by musical key, sleepy touch by sleepy touch.

The perfection of the afternoon's poplars blesses the air.

Possessed by passions, under the wing of a bird, we died three days ago.

The Ides of October

I paid for all the happiness that was bestowed upon us by the Ides of October.

I used to feel the presence of the child all around me.

A woman said I should pick a piece of slough cast by a snake and wear it against my skin.

I did it.

Flushed as a young peach, every sunset became a resurrection.

Roses wrapped around my waist, and later in June, the child was born.

A new October sets our pictures on the Spanish chest.

Emotions animate your cheeks.

Every night above the trees, the moon nurses the stars.

When I see cocoons of the larvae, I think silk as soft as the hair of the child.

When I say I love you, I think death as the harbinger of birth.

Your lips tremble, and your voice flattens.

I know you love me.

With nude fingers, the Ides of October betroth us again.

[Ides as the 15th day in March, May, July, and October according to the Roman calendar]

The Train to Vienna

let's take the train and go to Vienna
rent a room for a night and then waltz
in your arms the waist of the night trembles
fingertips touch a blue door which is locked
I sit barefoot on the floor
the windows' eyelashes are yellow and drunk
your voice moves stones in a lonely graveyard
to bury the tears I cry
and lonely like children of war
we cut in two the same pain for one night
you, the kiss of the love that could be
I, the rhythm of three beats in each bar
in Prater Park they sell lollipops
years pass by in one night
I rest my head on your shoulder
the train to Vienna has stopped

Fight

Purple roots cover all trails that go to the foothills.
Veins that the earth pushed to the surface.
I smell lavender.
Your words grow in the breeze like dough under the whispers of
the moon.
For three thousand years, sung by the poets of this land,
the naked shoulder of the mountain reigned in stillness.
The sky made itself invisible into a wooden box where my
grandmother kept her rings:
memories of loves that now fit in a small chamber.
The sea and the afternoon's breaths eclipse the taste of your colors.
The blue that slipped between the same branches of the old poplar
tree
stares me in the eyes.
Clouds ossify the fight of the earth against the earth.
Between my palms the body of a thin yellow candle.
I remember walking on a street where children were hungry and
had no shoes.
I took my shoes off and wiped my tears with the back of my palms.
Under my eyes, the skin became red and rough.
I wrote *I love you* on your left cheek.
I threw all the silver coins I had onto the dust of the street.
They were meant for the dead.
Let them help the living.
I remember your hand caressing the silk of my dress.
I purge all memories except one that belongs to the future.
You and I chanting to the incarnation of love under a tree on the
island where I was born.
The island where it is always spring, and the earth that does not
fight against the earth.
Did I tell you I was born on an island?

The Last Love

I eat macaroons in the same coffee shop
Roberto's guitar sells cheap dreams by the sea
young girls are ready for harvest like flowers of lust
I laugh…
I scratch poetry on a glass
I say the first love is French
you ask how's the last
it smells raspberries, vanilla, and grass
you touch my left wrist
I play a few cards
red flowers bloom on your cheeks
your teeth peel the skin of my gloves
you walk into darkness
I seal you in wax
how's the last love?
pray…
you shouldn't have asked

The Sea Becomes the Word

You and I dressed in white in a marble hallway.
The sunset bleeds under the skin of my chest.
Yellow turns to red.
The autumn blesses my forehead with the light oil of the last rose.
Your kisses hide in my hair.
Behind your eyes, the echoes of the marble hallway rain black sand.
It's evening.
Barefoot I walk to a small church at the margins of the city.
Your memory withdraws in a single spiral shell.
The flight of a bird opens the doors toward the eternity of the sea.
The word is the sea, and the sea becomes the word.
Nymphs' laughter in a nearby forest.
It's morning.
Where are you?

Exiled

You, evening of ours, how beautifully your lips tasted,
stars in your unbraided hair spread over still waters like lily pads,
rosy skin like the flesh of a pink grapefruit freshly open.
I still can breathe in your aromas of cherry-flavored cigars and
sleepless expectations.

Exiled under this oak tree, blue shadows under my eyes,
I think of him waiting for me in that place
where the sky meets the green of the grass and flowers bathe in
clear rivers.
Exiled by my own will, lizards running at my feet, I wait for the
pain to stop.
It never does.

Holding Your Hand

I walk through the future holding your hand
Barefoot I pray to a God whose name I don't know
The rain washes our hearts engraved in the wood
The child is the flower of tears and of sweet blood
It's not love that we want
It's the resurrection of dead
The breaths that the sea kills with her looks
Your hands and the sin we will never commit
The room that we rented is empty and cold
You know that I came
You feel that I left
I hear your voice
Black coffee waits for the sunrise of us
And the future runs in the past

You in Another Life

I fast for nine mornings. On the tenth, I walk barefoot toward the water.

The sea nurses the shore like mothers nurse their new babies.

The smell of beach roses and that of salt and sand.

The breeze plays on my neck and undoes the ribbons of my dress.

A wave washes on my body looking for forever; veins filled with my blood which has no expiration date.

I love for nine nights. On the tenth, I look for my future in a book that I open by chance.

Prophets, bones buried in the ground, unintelligible words, the pattern of kisses you left on my skin.

Shadows tremble on the silence of the tombs like virgins under the touch of their first lover.

I told you. He who knows me knows the darkness.

I am the ambivalence of form located above and below.

I am you in another life.

The Forgotten Syllable

I have an indefeasible desire
to make a fetish of the loves
that agonize under the temple
I am prepared to dance at your feasts
to be anointed by the grace of tears
I am neither a gift
nor something you can keep
I am the syllable forgotten on your lip

Contrary

Late afternoon.
Heated streets.
On my left, red shapes of lips on the walls.
On my right, a few bodies looking for shade.
A white bird flies over the tower of the church.
A boy tries to bring it down with a stone.
Inside the supermarket, I see hate in the eyes of two men.
That makes me think that perhaps the contrary of any type of galaxy is hate.
Do I dare to ask what is the contrary of your love?
I gave you one single tin soldier. You grew thousands of them.
Led by you, there is now an entire army trying to keep every soul away from me.
As though love for one soul requires the destruction of all others.
In the end, the boy brought down the bird.
Hurt, she falls in the sand.

Love Numbers

You used to identify the beating of my heart according to the phases of the moon.

The tonalities of my voice were symbolized by the heaviness of wheat in any given year.

We laid in the grass, shadows of poppies playing on our faces with the same rhythmicity of the waves on tranquil days.

At times we could feel the pulse of the new grains.

The line of my décolleté – as you used to say – nothing else but the demarcation between inexorable sins and the blushing tones of the sunsets.

The wind tasted like mulberries.

The Southern Pampas of Buenos Aires.

At the time it was one thing that I could not figure out.

What was the relationship between our love and numbers?

Were we one, were we two, were we three, or perhaps more?

How many were buried beneath our passion or by our passion?

Should we have counted us in?

I Wanted to Love You

each word I write cries on the tunes of spring,
a spring that ends in graveyards and in dreams
the night I abandoned you on that bench and left
snows in my mind the syllable of hell
I wanted to return
I wanted to love you
I choked on ecstasies from vaguely bluish lands
that night I took a part of you with me
I cashed your soul and threw it to some dirty lips
I bought one ticket from a shaman dressed in red
and flew towards the island of nowhere
and now between the mighty heaven and the hell
I love you, and I hate you are the same
and I return to find the pardon of the sands
to kiss your dust left on your mother's hand
I dress in colored ashes and black skirts
the language of the prophets with no tongues
on a new bench, I sit alone at funerals
and wait until the sea closes its eyes
to resurrect the ghost of love that you inscribed
on the red bridge between your spring and mine
I wanted to return
I wanted to love you

Bloom

you cut a piece of my hair
it curls between your index finger and your thumb
in the distance
silhouetted against the snow
knotted kerchiefs
the dress of a woman who insinuates herself on people's skin like
mold on walls
in the little house hidden by oak trees
in the unmade bed where every night you sleep alone
I listen to the mineral eyes of a saint
between your palms
the *Little Prince* plays with white plumes
signs that birds exist
the winter buries us deep in the ground
dissolved
our bodies gestate until the birth of spring
when on the top of an unspoken hill
you and I will bloom
into two trees whose fruit will feed the children of the world

Moonlight Love

Bones, blood, flesh trapped in brilliant moonlight.

The sand of the shore carried faraway by translucent tongues of water.

Around me, the mint grows taller than the trees; lassitude turning from gold to red.

Eyes become the locus where the desert and the sea meet.

Imprinted on my body the number twelve; the twelve horses of the sun-chariot.

He, the seller of time, looks at me.

His voice penetrates the membranes of my cells.

One hour of impossible love for two dimes.

I, who can foresee the future, buy.

The hour wraps around my hips like a passion vine around a tree.

For a second, you, the lover of the visible world, hesitate.

Streets inundated by the sweet smell of citrus.

Arms hugging a void.

You cannot eat that citrus, and you cannot touch me.

Moonlight love, remind me, why did I buy you?

Lilies of the Valley

I can see the woman who assumes things. Every night she picks the flowers that I throw on the road: withered lilies of the valley. She wants to be me. She wants my blood. She does not know I rearranged the bell-shaped whites so no one else can breathe their sweet scents. No one else can be me. No one else can make you, you.

The woman puts the withered flowers in her bag.
A new moon rises over her left shoulder. Bad luck.
I shiver.
I rush to protect her.
I stumble.
Before he died my father said:
If you try to do justice to the wicked, you will forget to do justice to the virtuous. And if you forget to do justice to the virtuous, you only work for yourself. That is the biggest sin of all.

I must think again.

September Tango

your tired feet have walked the desert
thorns and thistles scarred your skin
squirming in a mire
enraged by liars
your nights of passions
felt like the apocalypse

you, bearer of the bleeding hearts
I lock the door
I toss the key out of the window
I drink the sweetest wine
and listen to
the chants of prayers from the faraway Corinth

the walls are gray
the music plays
a yellow sunset lingers on my dress
September speaks
with lips of *tango nuevo*
with cords of harems with no keys

you, my adulterated love
I light your fire
blindfolded I seek a buyer
for all my sins
for this September blood that I resold
and for the girl who once was me

Adiós

Drops of you and me in the winter of our love.

Beneath my vocal cords, fingers knead the tongues of your kisses with the smell of wine.

Our souls dismembered by pasts that do not intersect; creators of a love as elusive as my adiós.

Tea leaves tell our future.

Your steps hang in the streets like the breasts of the earth under a bittersweet sky.

Your face grows washerwoman skin.

The land imprisons me.

I cry.

Tears of the sea.

You and I.

Czech Love

we ate Czech goulash and dumplings
drank Pilsner and smoked cigarettes
in a garden by St. Nicholas Church
I dragged you with me on a bench
your skin and your kisses were fresh
contouring each other: bark and heartwood
awe-struck we stood
bowed when love came
I saw what one sees in the light
you felt what one feels in the dark
it smelled of linden trees and drizzled confetti
we tied our wrists with ropes made of blood
buried our hearts in mountains and rivers
whisper the soul of the seventeen bridges
died the next morning in front of the Castle
and in the City of the Thousand Spires
not even the pigeons noticed a thing

If Only... Autumn

If only I could put my palm into yours for one single sunset
when the autumn's fingers smell corn silk,
and the eyelids of the sea cast spells on the cheeks of the stars.
Bathe with me at the end of the shore
where milk foam washes the feet of the children
and leaves traces of white shivers.
A pink conch tolls the waves announcing the homecoming of the
chrysanthemums.
The pain of birth leaks prayers on your lips
like half-naked Sundays leak monotony and coolness
on the yellow walls of the old city.
From the other side of your naked eyes,
I gather your tears in a wicker basket.
Laurel leaves hide under your pillow.
If only...
Autumn...

Son of the Desert

oh, let the summer come and go
wrapped into my dreams
coiling on your pillow
son of the desert
you look like the founder of gods
eyes hunt the cracks of pyramids
sands nest in your folded lips
under your sight
my breasts blossom
voices of the children of the moon
cupped palms filled with tears
son of the desert
tonight
I play my notes
close to your skin

Sweetness

Scents of linden trees illuminated by an old oil lamp.
The night is me.
I am the night where love delights dwell.
Shed your skin and come with me where minutes melt like chocolate on the tongue of a child.
You, sweetness from beyond the body, what can one say about you?

Spring

White.
We drank two lemonades sweetened with honey at the old terrace
by the church.
My body arched like a branch under the heaviness of cherry fruit.
I read from a book by Odysseas Elytis.
You smiled and listened.
The skies sighed.
The bells tolled twice.
Flowers silhouetted against my blood.
Wishes blossomed in your sweat.
I anointed your kiss.

Later, in the autumn, you wrote.
"I am in love with you. I do not understand how it happened."
Neither do I.
I told you: that which is against our will is unjust.
I have no other answer.
Yet.

Self-Indulgence

The smell of freshly baked bread in the nights when the ocean howls.

The moon's eyes linger on my neck.

The kitchen is hot.

Your eyes rest on the buttons of my dress.

One eye faces the sacred.

The other craves for the profane.

I call into being the taste of that which is hidden below the existence.

Touches.

Self-indulgence.

The breath of a salty ocean on the skin.

Everything is here between primal and the infinity of possibilities: the epistemes of love; the essence of beauty; the whispers of a language you cannot understand.

You need me in your bones.

The moon needs me in her naked light.

Yellow

A red sky sews our hearts together.
The moon threads the needle.
She pricks her finger.
A yellow tear falls on my cheek.

The Child to Be

I cut my hair.
I put it in a bag made of white silk.
Skies succeed one another.
The third one descends upon me.
It's Wednesday, the day of red carnations.
Your blood vessels kill my dreams like algae blooms kill fish.
From Thursday - why are you one sky ahead of me? - your voice
curls in every cell of my body.

The child will be born face up. He will watch the stars on their way
to nowhere.
I shudder. My breath heaves. Milky moonlight descends upon my
breasts.
What child?

On Friday you reply.
The one we'll make when we meet on Sunday.
My nails dig into my left thigh. My blood smells like carnations. It
ought to be still Wednesday. It can't be Friday. Friday smells like
Rose de Grasse d'Or.

What are you talking about? We do not meet on Sundays. I sew
clothing on Sundays. In fact, we never meet.

Your voice comes from Monday.
Our child to be. The one who has a bishop as a grandfather. The
one you know no other love but ours can bore. The one who will
contemplate the stars on their way to nowhere.

I take my hair from the bag.
I start placing it back on my head.
It must be Tuesday.

The Violin of Love

The air is still like the minutes before confession.

The cloak shrouds me.

On the second breath of the Easter of Roses, I walk to the outskirts of your love.

A violin exults fires upon darkness.

In one single stoke, your passion consumes and shuns me.

The chambers of my heart resound.

Reds prevent you from understanding how much I love you.

Double stop.

Movements.

My eyes are the eyes of the Sphinx.

I wait.

Summer Love

That summer love burned us until our skin became tranquilized.
We were ready to receive.
None of us cared about the danger of the thousand apples from which we bit.
Poetry?
Oh, poetry was too good to be read.
We tasted it and ate it with silver spoons.
All filtrations of the mind and senses hid in small apple bites and scented flowers.
By dusk, we exhausted everything with our breath.
The children's voices vanished into the dark.
The doubt of too much spilled between us like ashes from a broken urn.
Summer love.

Dark Love

green, you smell with your tongue
your thoughts pollinate mine
your fingers endanger the sailors
water which opens its lips and drinks them
ah, hour of man
when did you become the hour of horrors?
a book cover reads: Dictionary of Superstitions
I see the girl who tears out the heart of the pigeon
white feathers and blood spasm under the moon
the man she loves will marry her
in the street of the tall Cyprus trees and small mandarins
we meet
you give me a pigeon blood ruby
superstition,
I think of dying
dying without you knowing me
I touch with my cheeks the walls that you touched
adrenalized you think of me
your skin calls my name

love
dark love
with pins in his heart the pigeon still flies

Destined to Replace

The city and her languorous afternoon we spent in bed.
Every evening at 6 pm, the chords of your guitar used to grow rosebuds.
Sheer sunsets imprinted on our bodies.
Streets, labyrinths of gray cobblestones, dying in the orange light only to be revived later in the night by the steps of lovers desperately calling each other like song sparrows, brown streaks through each eye.

You said if I leave, I would become a stranger to the city. Did you mean to your lips?
I looked at the clock. Its hands showed no time. I answered:
How interesting. Strangers are always destined to replace.
By the little colored stall where ice cream was sold in the summer, your guitar shed its notes: rose petals in the remnants of a cold wind.

Indulgence

Skeletal fragments of coral and mollusks glued by calcite.
Limestone giving birth to grays, beige, and blue.
Your eyes as green as the grass on the dewy morning when
slithering snakes were driven into the sea.

Tears on your cheeks. I wipe them with my palms.
The desire to rebuild your soul. I cannot stop it. I am like those
women who think that their naked thighs and transparent negligées
can fix a broken heart. In fact, I am worse than them. I think I can
fix your soul.

I love you. Yet, my instincts are those of a simple worshiper of
reality. There is no sanctity in them.
Oh, indulgence of the self, how ignorant we are.

Night Poem

my love
my tears wed the earth
the night is naked, and it's drunk
it dances around roses
with lips which taste old wine
he who wins the night wins me
the many games of life
birds whose flight has stopped
sedated
the night's a carousel
which turns inside my heart

Sahara

The water bucket was brought by a woman.
She left.
Her child needed to be fed.
Sands.
The time comes from nowhere and goes nowhere.
Between my thirst and this bucket of water,
Between the consciousness of man and that of the stars,
Matter passes from blue to gold.
Sahara
Tonight
Your love gives way to his.

In This Pink Summer of Jaipur

in this pink summer of Jaipur
dressed in silk and in monsoonal dances
choked by smoke
forgotten by lovers
the nuances in which you speak my name sound hollow
the little girl
has only a grain of rice
she does not eat tonight
she exchanges her grain
for the fullness of pale stars

One I love you

my hair touches my shoulders
eyes, disheveled by the desperation of the stars, turn black
chords, those mistresses of love, of adulation, and of ardor
shadows
in the dark my chest wants to explode
psychosis, I hear what others cannot see
fingers, the hurricane of passion plays
a violin
a look
one I love you
that at the end
I knew you'd say

In the Dark, A Rose

Scars left by the teeth of the soul.
A dove turns black.
A crow turns white.
Inversion.
A serpent coils around a tree.
No daylight left.
I say I love you, and I lift my eyes toward the moon.
In the dark, a rose contours the shape of my left thigh.
Oh, you are here.
I thought so.

Phantasmagoria

You made a doll and projected your soul into it.
You named it after me.
Oh, your infantile state filled with rage and creativity.
In the end, the earth devours us.
If you give me that doll, I promise, I will show you that we are the planetary twin-peaked mountains.

From black through red through gold, we will ascend to the sky ending in the exact point where the universe blessed our love.

Our cross will bear fruits.
Can you see the fruits?
Their skin is humid, and their eyes are filled with desires.
Their colors are as vivid as the colors of your dreams.
I love you. Does it surprise you?
Now, please, give me that doll.

The Second Waltz

you say good morning
and I say not now
your eyes are thirsty like a drying well
you say I love you
and I say please wait
your kisses fall under the bracelets from my wrist
my heart is beating in your chest
I have to go
you want to talk to me?
perhaps another day
you know, another day will bring another night
why don't you write to me?
will I come back?

my love,
in front of all these icons that you brought for me in Crete
I swear I'll die again with you
inside the beauty of the second waltz
where we discovered our innocence
one chord per bar

Why?

The hypnotic red of the flowerpots molded in blood.
Dissimulation of an afternoon sacrifice.
An excruciating sunset crosses its fingers.
I tempt fate.
I see the child.
Toys forgotten in the sands.
A yellow like the aroma of the corn on the cob.
The sky dies in the convulsions of your "whys."
Why?

Your Love to Be

my words roam over your skin
your fingers roam around the craters of the moon
I rain blue scents of lovers from Hellada
I love you
I love with you
poplars break the morning sky
throw me to the sea...
it's afternoon
the time lights candles
on the shore a lace glove bleeds
secrets of the women of the water
you'll look for me
the virgin lip of an adulterated sea
your love to be

Reflection

The sky looked down into the waters and fell in love with itself.
I looked into my soul and fell in love with you.
Reflection.

Between the Sacred and Profane

the laughter of the symbolists
morbid
disoriented cries of birds
I pantomime seduction just for you
a naked shoulder, flowers, glossy lips
the lace of stockings lower than it should
I rip the left side of your shirt
you devour me with silver spoons
our love, twin-bladed axe between the sacred and profane
stolen from the forehead of a legendary ox
the promise of tomorrow
the promise that we'll meet
shadows of a painting signed Dali
both of us
children of the same insanity

It's March

it's March, and in the flower garden the time breaks into gigantic
fireballs
moths rotate around the golden light like mustard seeds in the cool
air
my hair grows long until it touches our naked ankles
I set the food on our wooden table
inside your eyes the spring sets scents of narcissuses and daisies
the valley blooms mauve tulips, eclipses of the heart,
by our mountain which is taller than the sky
love moves between your chest and mine
you kiss my cheeks
my hands tousle your hair
a smile from our non-existing past gazes at us
it smells naan and aromatic lamb
my dress is white; your shirt is dark,
I build from flowers our past until I cannot find its end
barefoot I stumble on old tears
are these the tears that you've cried?
an evil eye gets tangled in my hair
I hardly breathe
the evil eye now cuts my hair
in your arms,
you carry me on terraces made from your wildest fantasies
my dress is red, what happened to my dress?
your lips taste like mulberries,
mulberries from a tree which grew from the same root as my
childhood
there is pain somewhere between the two of us
is this what we call our past?

it's March, and in the flower garden the time breaks into gigantic
fireballs
moths rotate around the golden light like mustard seeds in the cool
air
you say I love you
my dress is white
your kiss is forged in fire and black passion

it's March
the March of our future and that of our past
Green
green
when you speak to me
when you speak through me
behind the dome of my forehead
poetry and wounded dew
the fragrance of my décolleté
eternally looking
only for you

The Biblical Sense of to Know

the biblical sense of to know
born in a summer that never existed
nailed to the cross of your poems
I'm losing my mind inside the blue night
I reach you in dreams you do not understand
It hurts when I'm there
It hurts when I'm not
I ask for the help gravediggers can grant
I wrote I love you on a note that I locked
It wasn't a snake, it was an iguana
the night the tango nuevo played its guitar
on fifteen decades I counted my prayers
my fingers were naked
my fingers were gloved

The Moon and I

In the green meadow by the lake,
the moon and I knit poetry of silk,
the language of the birds sleeps in the trees
like ripened fruits
your eyes are closed and faraway
the world rotates between two cherries and a kiss
stars rise over old memories of purple seas
like cherry buds
there was a glass of wine and an abyss
forgotten in the bloom of the first holy water
I tie your hands with ribbons made of dreams
I seal your chest with roses and with amber
oh, it's midnight and I must leave
yet not before
on your shaved face
the moon and I
drop dew
and virgin violets

The First I Love You

the moon is pregnant with desires
talismans caress your skin
naked shoulders dream

mirrors, phantoms of your thirst
passions hidden to the eye
chains pull you to me

between two whispers
I take you
to the land of the first I love you

And.. Love..

and...
this night is jasmine and is sand
the trees are fingers with no end
the earth has eyes
the tears have thighs

you…
you are the voice of lonely heights
I am the day without sights
a leaf is falling on my hips
into the air a form of lips

and…
your touches hide in poetry
a flower faints with jealousy
your dreams taste like forbidden fruits
the sea grows almonds and grows roots

yet…
the story didn't write its end
my eyes and yours are a blend
and…
love...

While You Sleep

while you sleep
right arm under your head
I catch a fish
in the marble net of the rustling stars
the morning comes with green leaves on her lips
my consciousness grows roots
it breaks through the asphalt of a cracked walkway
I used to play there when I was young
lose myself in the smell of oranges and paella that mama cooked
scratch my name on the old Spanish tiles of the courtyard
the jacaranda was in bloom
with my index finger
I cut my thoughts into pieces
from every cut, a multiplicity is born
the bed becomes too small
I lock my love in the adulterated red of an old wine
you turn your head toward the night we did not spend together
elegy
I turn my eyes toward the sky
and let the fish go

You and I

where is the book of poetry
that speaks of you and me?
born from a future time
in wonder
a baby star looks down
impermanence of flesh
remembrance of love
fresh sunsets settle
imaginary borders pass
while you and I
believe
the world's about us

Collage

I exist outside of my own existence.

Most hopes are beyond hope.

I am as insignificant as a drop of blood floating through the arteries of night.

Lost at sea the loneliness of sandcastles.

I can't love on behalf of others.

Collage two: One Life, Love, and Literature

How beautiful this winter would be if the sky were the color of your eyes.

A naked night knocked at the door. She wanted to buy love. I sent her away.

If I must pick one type of love, it wouldn't be eternal love.

Every morning I wake up to a list of things "to do." I hate things. I love only their meanings.

If heaven were hell, what would you do?

I do not speak anymore. Since I read Camilo José de Cela's *Cristo Versus Arizona* I decided silence is the only thing I should practice.

Love in Costa del Sol

this unbraided love of mine
its hair floats in the direction of a wavy afternoon
its body scatters over our summers spent in Costa del Sol
movements of our naked hands soaked in the sweet wines of
Málaga
afternoons invaded by saline waters and colored by colonies of fish
my lips moist
your shirt undone
the world an open rose
write me when the night smells lemon flowers and breaded fish
fried in olive oil
talk to me about the insanity of our passions
rhythms interrupted by the semi-circularity of arms
the bed is unmade
the cats purr
my dress is torn by the mysteries of waters that paint the eyes in
silver
I choke on the piety of my own words
on the strawberry taste of our *I love Yous* spoken in Costa del Sol
write to me

Bring the Summer

bring the summer back to me
to have and to hold
the flesh of sweet cherries
the fragrance of roses
when cotton candy sunsets sing
I'll deliver myself
in the arms of Morpheus
forever
and ever

The Promise of Us

The three days that we spent in that city.

The evenings, intoxicated by the smell of linden trees and the intimation of grace, entered our imaginations as the air fills a restless balloon.

Under the 7 am cold shower, the first morning blossomed into layers of rose and gold; shivering skin hoping for the warmth of a kiss.

The afternoons grew childbearing hips and spun them in the soft air; the *floreo* circularities of the flamenco dance.

Our candlelight dinners with their buttery taste, creamy textures, and oaked aged incantations.

The shell of our nights broken by mental possessions in front of which any other type of possession becomes superfluous.

I remember you holding in the air an unopen bottle of wine. Then, head on my knees, you cried.

Your tears trickled from my legs on the floor. The bed grew aromatic roots.

The promise of us, with its infinite ambiguity, spread through our bodies.

The city, like a gigantic swan, deserted its breeding nest.

It left us to the mercy of an inexplicable love.

Oh, yes, my love.

Oh, yes.

On Sacrifice and Meaning

Because I love you, I learned the meaning of sacrifice.
I reach in my pocket for a crooked old coin.
I sit in silence until the new moon rests on my right shoulder.
The crooked coin becomes liquid silver.
Its twelve shiny hands entangle in my hair.
A lonely ram runs in a field whose greens reach the sky.
It is autumn; an autumn that came too soon and whose suicidal breath brought dust and diseases.
The lamb will be born in the spring.
I cannot wait till then.
I try to advance, but the liquid silver pulls me back.
I cut its hands with a knife.
Every cut fulfills the dreams of the knife; my dreams are still in the waiting room.
A cricket chirps behind the chimney.
It's time to walk towards your soul.
I open the door of the waiting room.
I rub my cheeks with rosemary and wrap my body in the alphabet of love.
On my lips the unspoken words shine.
How beautiful they make me look.
The trail of a golden snail shows me the path to your soul.
I reach you.
I restore the degradation of our myth to its rightful fecundity.
The sacrifice becomes a festival, and the festival turns into creation.
I do not feed on things. I feed on their meanings.
The lamb will be born sooner.

The Orphic Egg

The builder of all things lives in me along with the seven disoriented ships he anchored in the port last spring.

The summer dried the sea. The wood of the ships got rotten.

The masts got buried in the wickedness of empty sunsets.

It is winter.

It is Wednesday.

I was in the washing room. I saw you folded my laundry.

In the library, the Orphic Egg suspends itself from the ceiling fan.

Under its pale light, I study my hands with the same precision the child studies his.

I shed my clothes as snakes shed their skin.

I feel your index finger contouring my spine.

One by one, your writings penetrate my mind.

The dimorphism of your poems spirals in two directions: torrential love and logical deductions.

They are both the product of your brain. I cannot kill them. I must allow them to exit.

The object of my poetry?

Not to concede life to touching pleasantries, fake passions, clichés, and the concentration of nothingness.

I displace the dark for the benefit of light.

I am the Orphic Egg.

Your fingers unbraid my hair, and your breath touches my neck.

My silhouette dissolves itself into the coldness of the seven ships.

It is Wednesday.

It is winter.

Prayer

you, fountain of youth,
forgive me
I am the one made from mud and from the skin of Attica's flutes
at night, my existence feels like an impertinence or perhaps like an
interlinear
a language half-imagined
half adulterated
by the bloom of the olive trees under the sticky wing of an angel
I was born in the swamps where the tombs of the prophets sunk
I am blood and bones when I smell the sea and the meat from the
grill
church bell toll and speak of death, and of the mystique of oblique
winds
you, goddess of youth,
source of life from where four rivers flow
your child-like body
stands some days on the top of the mountains
and others on the top of the fountains
your skin is dewed and flowered with love
my skin haunts the night of the deserts
your destiny is that of the innocents
mine is that of the sinners
forgive me, you, Hebe
that I do not ask for the gift of youth
give it to the children
give it to the sick
and throw what is left into the sea
the fish will be happy

A Night of Marble and of Gingerbread

on the top of the mountain
the pines silhouette against the whisper of the rocks
the night is cut from marble, and from gingerbread
the wind stops on a branch touched by a naked star
I take the measure of that which forever youth gives
red poppies that never whither
seeds that never impregnate the ground
a love that still plays with toys,
and lights candles in a Christmas tree in the middle of summer
the moon is mortal and concerned with trivial matters
and so am I
Hebe,
how many know that you are the bud of incest and patricide?
how many know your child eyes witnessed so many crimes?
filled with pain, you stop growing up, isn't is so?
oh, don't cry
here is my impermanent heart
wear it for one day
in the morning you will see the old oak dying in the rain
at noon butterflies will sit on your hair
in the night a Lethean forgetfulness will lecture on the beauty of
transitory love
kisses will feel like honey on the tongue
the breath of love will rest on your skin
you will grow up
what?
you do not want your forever youth back?
dream
it's spring

Rain

it rains on us
love expulsion from the womb of the moon
I wear the rustle of the Lyon silks
the silence of the swollen rivers
heavy like a giant snail

Kerf Cuts

kerf cuts your words left in my heart
a moon tear falls on my cheek
a rose hides its face
I sigh
you did not notice our hearts were sewed

Poetic Prose

My Name is Gabriela

My name is Gabriela. Papa used to call me Marie. Nobody understood why. Mama believed that Marie was the secret name of his mother, who was an actress. As far as I know, my grandmother's name was Lucrecia, and she was no actress. She was born into a religious family. Her uncle was a bishop. I have no idea how Mama came up with this story about my grandmother being an actress and having a secret name.

I cannot write anymore. If you want me to do it, you will have to lock me in the library. Only there silences become words, and words become soft and puffy like two humongous winter breasts glowing in the last rays of a sweet and sticky sunset.

Yesterday, I got lost in the sacrality of the winter carnival with its colors and aromas of musicality, and its hands of poetry extended to the moon and beyond.

Oh, no, you locked the library door.

I start knotting the thin rosy bodies of the quiet words that make the four thousand volumes that reside in here. An aerial bridge extends over the world. Dressed in a full-moon regalia, I walk on it. Around me, birds amalgamate the winds of the North with those of the South. I see stars floating on the seas. Blue meadows wave to me.

I cry. My tears reach the earth, and each and one of them grows into a new poem.

My name is Gabriela. Papa used to call me Marie....

Neurosis

I suspect I suffer from an acute crisis of half-bloomed neurosis. My past emotions do not fully interfere with my current experiences. The converse is true too. No sophistry added. How boring.

I jump in the water dressed in black lingerie made from Calais laces and Lyon silks. I can feel the waves pounding my body while my mind drowns in the ambiguity of the French Nouveau Roman standing mid-way between modernism and post-modernism like a drunken sunset that cannot distinguish between yellow and orange.

The foliage of the sea turns burgundy. Your fingers contour my face.

Oh, you.

I forget that my favorite poet is Arthur Rimbaud with his "A thousand Dreams within me softly burn" and "I shed more tears than God could ever have required." All I remember is that once I wrote: "I've never existed outside of your obsession with me and my interpretations of you." There is something about these interpretations that make you burst in cascades of laughter and *art* your love for me with lust.

One morning, left by my pillow, I found your reply written on a large index card: "I had to bury your existence inside my obsessions. If not, your love could not have been fully stabilized. You above anyone else know that an absolute correspondence in love does not exist. Love is a mathematical singularity."

A wet little bird shivers in my palms. The foliage of the sea turns darker.

Your fingers contour the back of my neck.

My eyes catch fire.

Night, have mercy on us.

On Women's Writings

I do not like women's writings. They talk too much about their bodies.

Notice the negative connotation attributed to the relationship body/femininity construed as an obstacle to the evolution of the spirit? This man's feeble mind has confined women to lands of sensuality, magic, swamps, and mud; in short, to categories related to the carnal. Women can only be aware of tumultuous feelings that erupt inside their bodies. Nothing else. There was an implicit juxtaposition between body/femininity and spirit/masculinity, the latter understood as superior.

I navigated the incredible writings of women like Virginia Woolf, George Sand, Marguerite Yourcenar, and many others.

I became a mirror. I produce images of the spirit and of the body.

I play with them. I absorb them. I devour them.

I am the same with the richness of the intellect and the opulence of feelings.

My body is the alphabet of a language spoken at the exact hour when the sunset rains its cherry blossoms over the laughter of children.

I love the frenzy of the 1920s. Oh, *les années folles*!

I am the quintessence of that which you will always desire.

I am a woman.

I am not made in your image.

You are made in mine.

On Poetry and Daffodils

My poetry is neither the chronicle of my sufferings nor the chronicle of my loves as many seem to believe. It does not contain the description of my marital status nor that of my accomplishments. It does not record my joys or my passions with the precision of a timeclock. It does not dwell in my sadness. Sadness is the place where I dwell when I write the word *sea* , and I cannot understand its meaning the way Elytis understood it. I was not born in Hellada. I can use that as an excuse for my poetic inadequacies.

My poetry is that which comes from the realm of the unfulfilled. It is the echo of the waves that you can guess but cannot see because they are not born yet. It is the voice of the blood that dries on the feet of the prophets. It is the dream of my cheeks that you will never touch. My poetry is the body of a Sunday that forgot to put walnuts and cinnamon in its baklava. It is the promise of tomorrow.

Three years ago, I bought a silver icon at an auction. The icon belonged to the M. family. They used to be one of the most preeminent families on the island of Crete. Hellada was tattooed in my non-Hellenistic soul by the will of my parents, not by mine. You cannot stage a coup against your own baptism when you are four months old.

I was in love in Hellada. So much for "Let's fall in love in Spain." Every time the church bells tolled, he, the one who loved me, used to bring me daffodils. One daffodil for each bell toll. When the church bells stopped tolling, I had so many daffodils that I could not carry them anymore. I had to let them fall on the ground.

I ran and I took the first ship out of Piraeus.

Until this day he — the one who loves me — still waits for the girl that will keep his daffodils and marry him.

Of course, he does. There is always the promise of tomorrow. There is always my poetry and there is always one more night of passion.

Of Wounds

I cannot tell which of the wounds I acquired hurts more. I gather all of them in a large wicker basket and sort them out every summer morning when fields are filled with lavender and roses.

During autumn nights, while I listen to the wind unbraiding the old oak trees, I re-live each of them.

I see how the Lie walks hand in hand with the Betrayal, and how the Betrayal indulges herself in the sweetest of wine. Oh, that irresistible taste of black grapes that melts in her mouth. It almost makes her attractive.

The Envy wears red lipstick and high heels. She dances naked on a wooden table. At every turn, she spreads poisonous confetti in the air, and she lowers her eyes. I try to decipher the meaning of her gestures. I cannot.

The Greed, with her childbearing hips, indulges herself with poor souls who live at the margins of the city. The children are hungry, and the mother is long exhausted. The beds are cold, and the moonlight enters the rooms through broken windows.

I feel the pulse in my temples. Exhausted I go over the meaning of love and sacrifice. I try to restore them in their right place.

Love and sacrifice are the consummation of all acts that lead to the warm meal that one hands to an old man who dwells in the streets during cold winters. They are the sum of all unknowns. They are the fingers that draw the light of stars in the darkest of the skies.

The Blue Jay's Feather

Winter.

The day after Miriam left for Europe.

A blue jay looks for food on the cracked asphalt of the street, long rows of dark buildings, cadaverous trees, dilapidated fences. The city's noises vanish in a moribund sun.

I am in a building. A paraffin lamp burns on a round glass table. The light trickles on the walls like water.

There is something familiar about this room; the vague scent of dried flowers and the tear-like motif on the walls.

I can hear footsteps coming from upstairs. In a flash my heart goes into my throat.

I whisper.

"Miguel, let's get out of here."

He put his hand over my month.

Laughter comes from upstairs. It is Jacques' laughter. His and the laughter of a woman. She is not Miriam. It cannot be her. Miriam left yesterday. What am I thinking? The laughter cannot be Jacques' either. He is dead. Jacques is dead.

The smell of the room invades my nostrils again. I know now. It is the smell of the dried flowers that Miriam put on Jacques' coffin on the day of his funeral.

My mind freezes.

After an age, a terrifying scream tears the air apart. The room feels like a tomb. I pull away from Miguel's arms, my soul dark, and the tightness in my throat stronger. In a mirror I replace my image with that of my grandmother.

I whisper in a voice that is not mine.

"Miguel, with you or without you, I am getting out of here."

He bites his upper lip.

"Clara, how many times have you asked me for the truth?"

"Right now, I do not need the truth. I want to get out of here. There are dead people in here, or ghosts, or whatever. I want out."

The light from his eyes vanishes. He shivers.

"Clara…. Listen…"

The geometry of the space changes. Whirlpools of colors contort their translucent bodies under my eyes.

Through a little square cut from nothingness, I see a lonely blue jay feather floating in the sky.

Paraffin and dried flowers.

Butterflies Always Die

In times of fortune and misfortune, I am always at the mercy of silence. Perhaps because I was born on an island where seldom does anything happen.

Yesterday the water and the light invaded my tongue's buds, and I was forced to look at myself upside down. I could see the splendor of a naked butterfly ready to mate. Do you know for how long do two butterflies stay together? Sixteen hours. The exact time we spent together in the silence of the island.

Suspended in the between time, neither of us moved. No cosmic sacrifice happened. No driving force was brought to life. No blood interfered between two consecutive breaths.

Everything was nothing else but the crisp silence of the light. The mystery of that you can see with your own eyes and touch with your own soul. No spots of dark. For the first time we decided to seek the mysterious in the light and not in darkness.

Behind the clarity of your face, my face appeared, then yours came behind the clarity of mine, and everything went like this like in a surrealist dream inverted upon itself.

At the end of the sixteen hours the sea washed us away.

I forgot to tell you.
Butterflies always die.

The Six O'clock Café

The night had too many eyes, too many tears, and too many candles. It left sticky traces of wax in our souls. Escaped from its unbearable seduction, the morning light felt like a benediction: the smell of fresh brewed coffee; the whiteness of the tablecloth; the raspberry cobblers aligned on the window of the freezer; your eyes clearer than any mountain spring ever known.

We finished our coffees. Christina, the waitress, blew us a kiss and then threw her hands in the air. Her high-pitched voice rang in my ears:

"Don't forget to come back to the Six O'clock Café, you, love birds."

"We will be back tomorrow."

Through the windows, I saw the trolley moving like a red sleepwalking worm. We rushed out.

Side by side from our chairs, we watched the city and the sea coming to life. It was a bridal time filled with the smell of salt and of sweet oranges. Your lips trembled, and you spoke about our wedding.

We were going to get married on a boat. We would leave the shore on a Sunday morning. Behind us, all church bells would toll. I was going to wear a simple dress made from hemp, and a crown of pink fresh roses gathered the midnight before our marriage when the moon was rising from the waters. A huge basket filled with a thousand cherries would be set at our feet to make our marriage as sweet as their flesh. Blue and white threads wrapped around our wrists would protect us forever.

The end of the line.

How did we end up at the Six O'clock Café again? The trolley must have gone in a circle. We laughed, got off the trolley, and entered the place.

I thought everything looked strange. The refrigerator was now on the other wall. The tablecloths were not white anymore. A long-faced waiter passed me.

I asked:

"Is Christina here?"

"Christina? Oh, Christina quit working here five years ago."

Numb, I looked at you. There was something deeper than desperation in your eyes. Something that I could not translate.

Your arms pull me to your chest. I could hear your whisper.

"Please tell me we are married."

I looked at my fingers. I had no wedding band.

Autumn Reflections

I walked on the street between the two rows of those old homes with their locked doors, their blue peeling walls, and their sleepy eyes concealed by dark brocade drapes.

I wanted you.

First, the song seemed to come out of nowhere. Then on the opposite sidewalk, I could see the children dressed in white, blindfolded, their feet floating above the cracked asphalt like some withered autumn leaves carried by a psychedelic wind.

The children sang. I could make out the refrain: "We can't see, we can't hear."

Was I dreaming?

During autumn, I dream. That is because I was born in autumn on a day that has no saint assigned. Therefore, every year, on my birthday, I make up things.

You waited for me at the end of the road. I felt your hungry fingers unbuttoning my raincoat.

The children approached. Their little voices pinched my brain like needles. Their thin bodies reflected in your blue eyes.

I asked:

Can you see the children?

What children?

The children dressed in white. They are in your eyes. Why can't you see them?

Your fingers continued to unbutton my raincoat.

Lord, I must have been born on the day of children who cannot be seen and cannot be heard.

I choked.

Shadows

My indecipherable shadow on that faraway beach. You talked to it.

I did not hear what you said because I wasn't there. I was in the cemetery looking for a grave. I couldn't find it.

Name after name stuck on crosses.

Trophies of death lurking in the heat like carcasses hanging on a rail.

Concentrated flavors of withered roses.

I am telling you I went to the wrong cemetery. My feet got puffy. Was I wearing somebody else's shoes?

The sunset lifted me in the air.

Good, I thought. Now, perhaps I could find the grave. I looked down and instead I saw shadows dancing on the top of each cross. I searched for my own. It wasn't there.

Ah, now I remember.

First, you kept my shadow with you on the beach.

Later you buried it into the ocean's waves.

You did it, didn't you?

Who Am I?

For five times in twenty-four hours, I face in the direction of the sea.

The first time the morning star floats above the water as innocent as the breast of a young girl. Soon the sun will try to catch her naked and burn her skin. She will escape. Pigeons will carry her across the sea. She will melt into yellow waters. Her last rays will fall in my lap like feathers.

I will rejoice.

The second time, divorced from her night bed, the light disperses itself on the shore. I can see myself washing clothes in the sea. My hair is tied in a ponytail. I am barefoot, and my dress is rolled up. The skin of my lips is cracked. I bleed. The clothes I wash smell cedar and spices. The shadow of a seagull positions itself on my forehead. The sea reflects the twelve signs of the zodiac. I can see no relationship between my destiny and that which I do. I am scared.

At noon, the sun kneads the waters with rapture. Shells shed pearls on the shore. My own rational thought leaves my body. I delight in the waves like a gazelle in the grasslands. I feel the movement of the water on my skin. Its cyclical quality sends me in a state of ecstasy. No, it is not the ecstasy of Saint Teresa of Ávila. It is something similar to a soporific trance. I am dead, and I am alive at the same time. I come from the sea. I return to the sea.

In the afternoon, my rational self awakes. My mind spreads its wings. I get preoccupied with verbs. I set one triangle in the normal position, and I invert the other one. I bind them together. I make myself a dress from pieces of paper inscribed with old symbols. Oh, femininity! You are the goddess of vines, the mother earth, the chalice, the blood, the fertility of the womb. I mull over these desperate efforts to equalize the feminine with the masculine. There is nothing in these symbols that points to the intellect of a woman.

In the evening, the sky stretches itself from blue to dark violet. The silk of the gloves hugs my fingers. I feed my iguana with cookies soaked in champagne. She hisses at me. I open a package of silk stockings. The door opens by itself, and you step in. Then it closes. I stare at you. You are in by your own volition. One kiss and you borrow my tears. One touch, and I borrow your pain. A passage rite. I keep a coffin adorned with lilies in my bedroom. I sleep besides death like Sarah Bernhardt.

Did you hear that noise? A rosary fell from the Spanish chest.

The wind slips between the petals of a rose and opens it.

Who am I? If I knew, I would tell you.

Did you say you love me? The twenty-four hours are up. Nobody is facing in the direction of the sea anymore. There is no me.

In Defense of Emma Bovary

I love how you dress for weddings: the repetitive movements of your fingers when you knot your bow-tie and that splendid nakedness of the white rose on your lapel, a true *nuditas virtualis* that makes me dream of the birth of a god in the zodiacal sign of Virgo.

I miss the glow of your face in the candlelight, the vibration of the wine glass' crystal stem between your fingers, the memorable tunes of the waltz coiling around your senses.

It is dark. I lay on the sofa, and the smell of pain killers and sedatives dwells in my nostrils. I can hear the noise of the withered leaves coming from outside. It frightens me. The sweetness of the *nuditas virtualis* fades away. I think of Emma Bovary, the so-called narcissistic self-deluded character, the adulterous woman, the daydreamer, the *nuditas criminalis* par excellence.

How pathetic and enslaved by time our judgments are. If Emma were a man, she would have had the masculine license to thirst for the feminine. No judgements would have been passed. There is no masculine equivalent of Emma Bovary in literature. Profoundly telling, don't you think?

Emma committed the *mortal* sin of having affairs. She killed herself as self-punishment, we are told. How ignorant people who think so are. Turn the page and think of Emma as the woman who pitied the birth of her own daughter. Have you ever stopped to think why she would do that?

Those winds and the frightening noise of the withered leaves.

Where are you?

You do not visit anymore. You forgot your white rose on the head on my sofa. I need to tell you again. I love how you dress for weddings.

Creation

How beautiful you made my loneliness with your love letters and your ceaseless colors that burn my eyes every time I look at them.

I am forever in your power because I was brought into this world by your imagination. I am your creation.

I feed on the same sea that nursed us when we were children.

I am the glue that holds together the baked sands stuck on your skin during endless torrid summers.

Sometimes I look like a four-leaf clover sitting on the lapel of your black coat on the 15th of every month.

Other times when it is dark, you call me Selena, and you make my twelve fingers knead your ecstasies and plant them in whispering tombs.

Your desires are the stage on which I dance, my hair unbraided, my first youth gone, my death date undetermined yet.

I thought nothing was about me. Everything was about you and your mind with its powerful sounds of rapid waves and its one thousand boats anchored in the same port.

Yet at 9 am in the morning, you said something that made me believe you became possessed by your own creation.

Green deep waters.

Is that true?

Feminine Submissiveness

Feminine sexual scars: real, invented, and in some cases only dreamed. Wounds exposed in plain view in order to obtain something in exchange. If not justice, then sympathy. If not sympathy, then the attention of a certain male prototype.

A desperation to direct the masculine imagination toward the submissive feminine with its painful blows; blows exacerbated by the brutality of our patriarchal society. Yet something more was added to that: female purple skin calling for the asperity of males' touches, abandon, suggested nudity, swollen lips, tons of adjectives filled with a sickening excess of sweetness.
I remember him saying.

An entire arsenal of attraction built on wounds that should be sanctified not used to incite maleness. Those women hang their sexual lesions like paintings on walls for the sole purpose of giving males glimpses under their underwear.

C'mon. You know it.

I did not. However, he was a man of high intellect. It was difficult to go against him. I had to wait. I had to outmaneuver him.

So, I played my feminine submissive part. Add some madness to that and I am quite sure I looked like Ophelia running from room to room dressed in black negligees incapable of understanding my own distress. What a nightmare.

Was he right?

Dematerialization

It was a sort of dematerialization that left behind the scent of orange blossoms and the vague memory of sultry afternoons growing by the margins of the pond: those afternoons in need for seed germination. I am sure you can remember them.

You and your love for me which have always looked for my blood. I told you I am air and therefore I do not have a body. I fill the space in which other bodies manifest themselves.

I am every breath you take in your nights of love when you think you love other women. Have you ever noticed how blue and humid is the air you breathe between two kisses? That's me.

Oh, I agree. Sometimes I may look like plum lips, and other times like tiny specs of red wine sprinkled on your shirt. Those are the times when the moon is full, and the cicadas' wings listen to the vibrations coming from the membrane of their own abdomens.

It's summer: pink roses, fresh lips, quiet balconies.

May I have my black nightgown back? I want to feel its silkiness against my skin.

Oh, you are right.

I do not need it. I do not have a body.

Is it my imagination or your breath just got heavier?

He

He acted like what he *was*: one of the most handsome and wealthiest bankers of the city.

Nightly candlelight parties in his villa whose balconies opened toward the ocean. Château Mouton Rothschild Pauillac: deep reds and an unmistakable taste of eucalyptus. Coquilles Saint-Jacques, escargots, Provencal fish stew whose aroma imbibed the corridors from lazy late afternoons until early mornings when it was replaced by that of coffee and freshly baked croissants.

It was an act. He looked like a man who, while sleeping with one woman, thought of another. Teeth planted in warm lips in an eerie absentness of mind; nothing less than automatism. His entire being was consumed by something else, something as imperative as the birth of a child: the naked vision of a woman whom he could not have.

Of Light and Darkness

He stepped into a space governed by love and hate at the same time. He did not understand how these two concepts melted into each other by means of interplay.

Light and darkness adorning the shoulder of the woman who wakes up in the arms of her lover. There is no distinction between the two. Both mold the roundness of her shoulder with its naked softness and its distinct sharpness. During the nights in which the moon is glossy and crisp like the crust of a country bread, the woman's body gives birth to mountain chains and fragrant valleys.

The world remains the same as two lovers riveted onto themselves.

I know he loved me. Yet his mind was too pedestrian to understand.

Gnosticism

He was a gnostic par excellence. He loved Hellenistic Alexandria, a place where syncretism, with its unbelievable superposition of religions, grew like oyster mushrooms. Think fleshy greyish-brown, yellow, and pink colors, one on top of each other.

During winters, the ghosts of the Alexandrian carnival, inscribed in colored tiles, mesmerized him. They lived in his mind like relics in churches, wrapped in scents of myrrh, overwhelmed by veneration, buried under the kisses and the requests of those who believed in miracles.

Carnival: late Latin expression meaning *carne levare*, "remove meat." Some will say "farewell to meat."

Ah, the famous libertinism of Carpocrates. He did not believe in it. The sweetness of the flesh meant little to him. And I am coming to what you want to know, am I not? You want to know why he loved me so much and how he conceived of our relationship.

Turn around. Breathe the smell of grass growing on old tombs: tombs of saints, madmen, oracles. Remember, the wish to die is as natural as erotic impulses.

I will blindfold you. You will take your shirt off. I will drop on your chest the unadulterated coolness of the morning dew.

In silence I will shade my skin between the gates of heaven and those of hell. The sun will set on my plump and humid lips. You can touch my waist with the fingers of your right hand. You can go down to the middle of my left thigh. You cannot deviate. I am forever yours if the tip of your fingers can read the patterns inscribed on my thigh. Do it and I will kill his memory.

What is going to happen if you cannot read with the tip of your fingers? Oh, I've always believed that after death souls go to the moon.

Your call.

For crying out loud, I am joking. Stop looking at my legs.

I know you love me. He loved me too. I am who I am and who I am is hidden from view.

Now, can I get a drink from the bar? And really those devil eggs look so good.

It Was Not Love

I alternate deep and high-pitched tones; opposing predispositions of a breathing universe.

You favor discussions about T's novel. T was a mediocre writer. Yet he did capture a side of me that fascinates you; a side that looks like those apparitions reflected in the mirrors of our bedroom every night.

What brought T and me together?

It was not love. You know that.

Perhaps it was the knowledge that all combinations are fundamentally flawed.

Did you raise your eyebrows?

No. Don't touch me. I don't want to be thrown in the swimming pool anymore.

If I say I love you

In a flash, my mind shows me a thousand streets tormented by loneliness. These streets - once the grand winepresses of human bodies and cars - are now haunted by sickness and eaten by desolation.

It's spring. The ocean's water is warm like a country bread. I can taste it. The crisp crust, the sweetness of grains, and earth melt on my tongue.

I miss you and the chestnut tree from that pastel afternoon when we first kissed.
Why did I love you? Of course, you were handsome, but it wasn't that. I loved you because you could not have been conquered by the tricks with which a woman conquers most men. Why would I even want a man that any woman with lipstick and stilettos can have?

I am digressing, am I not?

It's spring. The water is red. Under the light of its pearls, flowers open like fresh young lips.
I avert my mind from the memory of your arms which tries to drag me inside an abyss of naked love; a love blessed with the force of the mistral and the sensuality of linked fingers under the moonlight.

The earth and the waters are one.

Yet the pain is heavy and filled with fluids like the chest cavity of a dead animal hanging upside down.

I can see your boat. It's beautiful.

The world is sick.

If I say I love you, will you tell me what I can do to heal it?

Love Games

I strolled along that large corridor whose walls were decorated with portraits: trophies of your love games. You fed on those loves, didn't you? You overextended. Overextension kills empires. I bet you didn't think that it could kill real love too.

Every night the fleshless arms of your love games crawl on you like fire ants.

I know misfortune when I see it.

I know it because I am not a saint.

Hope? If there is any left it must be on another corridor.

Follow me.

The Angel of God

He comes back only when the Angel of God makes blue and yellow rings fall asleep on my fingers.

One night he swore his oaths upon our unmade bed and the river Styx.

His guitar swore its oaths upon a red rose.

This is not the time of year when his tears - chariots of fire - fall from the sky.

Neither that day of spring when I lie in bed covered by wedding veils.

Those are the only times when his soul plays guitar behind the Japanese screen in my bedroom.

You couldn't hear him playing in the library.

So, what did you really hear?

Do you believe that his ghost hides inside his portrait hanging on the wall?

Oh, no! This is not a Harry Potter fantasy. His soul is not inside any portrait.

Now, I think it's time for you to leave.

Why? Are you asking me why?

You saw the inscription below his portrait: granted just a quote he loved.

There are only three things to be done with a woman. You can love her, suffer for her, or turn her into literature. *

Here's your answer. You can't do any of those things. So, you better leave.

No, his soul wasn't here tonight.

Tonight, it is I who speaks, not him.

*from Justine by Lawrence Durrell

Rien Que Pour Toi

Between the bed and the window, in that space that smells roses and *rien que pour toi*, the morning lets her hair down. She is so close that I can reach her skin with the tip of my fingers.
I know his book and the fame it brought him. The book in which he made me – the me that he imagined – the main character.

He was fascinated by the purple of my makeup and the yellows of my cobra, who used to erect the upper portion of her body to greet him every time he visited.

I do not know what demons he tried to exorcise. In the heat of those summer afternoons, he used to sip his sangria and attempt to find almost religious justifications for what he called *my ecstatic existence*; an existence populated with the richness and succulence of the Mediterranean literature and void of bullet points.

His acute shyness and his need to overcome the incapacity to love beyond nightly adventures used to ring in my ears like some unhinged marimba lamenting the loss of a pipe.

The dress that I wear in page twenty-seven. That dress and the heart-shaped red stone pierced with a hole I used to wrap around my neck. I found that stone in a churchyard. I was too young. Perhaps an older version of me would have made him a better writer. Do not laugh. You are too handsome when you laugh.

In the end, he managed to do something special. He invented the name of a perfume and made me wear it on every page of his book: *rien que pour toi*.

I hid his book somewhere in the library. Yet, every morning, in the space between the bed and the window, it still smells *rien que pour toi*.

Fame

It seems to me that we struggled to survive for thousands of years so that today each of us can have 30 seconds of fame.

Our latest accomplishment may be our last.

On Winning and Hate

The afternoon smelled of a brick wall; the wall I used to scratch with the knees and the nails on my way to the sea.

My blood-stained my socks and fed the roots of the orange tree mama planted one spring before my seventh birthday. Soon after, the tree grew blood oranges.

I used to dream I would reach the port before crickets would serenade the white cement between the bricks, and the evening wind would sew the wounds from the face of the wall.

I needed a God to lead me to the sea. In Mama's stories, there were too many Gods leading souls to heaven. I did not want to go to heaven. I wanted to go to the sea.

I used to fail. I did not understand what failure is. The next afternoon, little ducks embroidered on the rim of my light blue dress, I would start climbing the wall again.

One day I thought I would get to the port and run straight into the sea.

Little did I know that day came when I first looked into your eyes. The ghosts of your victories and those of your wounds flapped inside your retina like laundry left to dry on a wire. Long red poles floundered left and right like the wings of a moribund bird. The body of a boat eroded by salt, and by the kisses of the women of your past agonized in green and blue.

The sea inside your eyes: on the right your love for me, and on the left, your hate for the world.
Did I say *your love for me?* You see, over time, I had to reconsider that formulation. Your feelings resembled more a never-ending animal magnetism than love.

Let me make one thing clear. No one person is sufficient to drive all demons from another one. You can think Goethe's elective affinities if you wish. I cannot save you from you. You need to help me. I can carry this conversation into the night and win.

Ah, winning! The day I understood I can win, I stepped into hell.

That day was the day I lost my innocence and with that the paradise. Since then, my blood has never stained my socks anymore. The orange tree has never grown red-fleshed oranges, and Mama stopped telling stories.

I beg forgiveness every night.

Every night the number of my wins, and that of my enemies grows.

I became you as much as you became me.

Yet I know no hate. You do.

What's wrong with me?